ONE GLASS WALL

for Mum and Dad

Danusia Iwaszko

ONE GLASS WALL

OBERON BOOKS

LONDON

First published in 2004 by Oberon Books Ltd
521 Caledonian Road, London N7 9RH
Tel: 020 7607 3637 / Fax: 020 7607 3629
e-mail: oberon.books@btinternet.com
www.oberonbooks.com

A catalogue record for this book is available from the British
Library.

ISBN: 1 84002 526 3

CHARACTERS

MARK FREEMAN, Father

BRIDIE FREEMAN, Mother

MORAG FREEMAN, Daughter

The character of Morag, who ages from eight to sixteen, should be played by the same (adult) actress throughout.

One Glass Wall was first performed at Theatre 503 at the Latchmere on 2 November 2004, with the following cast:

BRIDIE, Siobhan McCarthy

MARK, John Cormack

MORAG, Lucie Dobbing

Director, Crispin Bonham Carter

Designer, Belle Mundy

Movement Director, Vanessa Mildenberg

Sound Designer, Nigel Piper

Lighting Designer, Adrian Mullan

Stage Manager, Rosie Gibson

Assistant Director, Melanie Branton

ACT 1

A Saturday afternoon in autumn 1968. Set in a Morris Minor. Dad, MARK, is driving with wife BRIDIE by his side. In the back seat is MORAG, their daughter, aged eight. MORAG is perched behind her parents, peering out from between their heads. MORAG and MARK are laughing.

BRIDIE: What's a cows-go?

MORAG: Oh, Mum…

MARK: Tell her again, Monkey.

MORAG: Knock, knock.

BRIDIE: Knock, knock.

MORAG: No, Mum, who's there!

BRIDIE: Who's there?

MORAG: Cows-go.

BRIDIE: Cows-go who?

MORAG: No, cows go mooooo! (*MARK and MORAG laugh.*)

BRIDIE: (*Not getting it.*) Oh… Oh, yes.

MARK: Very good, monkey. I'll tell them at the lab on Monday.

BRIDIE: What's a cows-go?

MARK: How long are we going to be stuck behind this caravan? (*He sings:*)
I'm Popeye the Sailor Man, I live in a caravan
I like to go swimming with all the bare women,
(*Guffaws from MORAG.*)
I'm Popeye the Sailor Man.
Toot toot!

MORAG: Do it again!

MARK: I'm Popeye the Sailor Man… (*He swings out to overtake.*)

MORAG: Don't go yet, Dad, there's a big lorry coming!

BRIDIE: Careful!

MARK: Oh, God! (*Pause.*) I can't wait for them to open the new bit of the M1. Three lanes of motorway all the way from Nottingham to Leeds.

BRIDIE: Three lanes!

MORAG: Wow! Like the roads in America!

MARK: Then we'll be motoring. No learner drivers, no bicycles and no children.

MORAG: No children?

MARK: Nope. At the start of the motorway there's going to be a little hut where you drop them off.

BRIDIE: I don't know if I approve.

MARK: That's the rule. No children under ten.

MORAG: I hate motorways!

MARK: There's a row of hooks in the hut, with shoe bags hanging on them and you pop your children in them.

MORAG: We won't drive on them, will we, Mum?

BRIDIE: No, darling.

MARK: And you can pick them up on your way home. Or you can choose a different child if you like!

MORAG: Oh, Dad, it's not true! (*She thumps him.*)

MARK: Morag! That's very dangerous!

BRIDIE: All right, calm down. Who'd like a nice tomato?

MORAG: Me, please, Mum.

BRIDIE: Here's a tissue. Don't get it everywhere. Mark?

MARK: No thanks.

MORAG: Are we there yet?

BRIDIE: It's a very long way, Morag, don't start asking if we're there yet.

MORAG: Is it as far as Loch Ness?

BRIDIE: I think so.

MORAG: I wish we could go to Loch Ness again.

MARK: Do you remember my photo of Loch Ness? Do you remember my black paper cut-out of the monster in front of it?

BRIDIE: I've still got the photo.

MARK: Rather convincing, if I say so myself.

MORAG: You showed it to next door and they thought it was real.

BRIDIE: I don't think they really believed it

MORAG: Yes they did!

MARK: He still goes on about it. He's so stupid!

MORAG: He's so stupid!

MARK: He's as thick as two short spanks!

MORAG: He's as thick as cold rice pudding!

MARK: He's as thick as porridge!

MORAG: He's as thick as woolly knickers!

BRIDIE: That's enough, Morag.

MORAG: Dad's saying it!

BRIDIE: Look at that lovely tree.

MORAG: What?

BRIDIE: That lovely big one there.

MORAG: He's as thick as cat poo.

BRIDIE: Morag!

MORAG: What?

BRIDIE: Where are the Green Shield stamps we got with the petrol, Mark?

MARK: In the glove compartment.

MORAG: (*Quietly.*) He's as thick as an elephant in the zoo.

BRIDIE: Nobody's listening, Morag. Is there a new book in here as well?

MORAG: (*Very quietly.*) He's as thick as a snail.

BRIDIE: Now, what are we going to get from the catalogue?

MORAG: Can I stick them in, mum?

BRIDIE: No.

MORAG: Oh, go on!

BRIDIE: Only if you stop saying those silly things and promise to be good.

MORAG: Promise.

BRIDIE: All right then.

MARK: How many books have we got?

BRIDIE: Five. Stick them in properly now, Morag. Straight lines.

MORAG: Yes.

BRIDIE: What about a new kettle?

MORAG: We don't need a new kettle, it's a waste of stamps.

MARK: What about something for the car?

MORAG: No. Let's get a toy! A friend for Geoffrey. (*Her stuffed rabbit.*) You'd like that wouldn't you, Geoffrey? It's not fair to have one little rabbit on its own. What's that Geoffrey? (*Geoffrey whispers in MORAG's ear.*) I know. He says he's very lonely.

BRIDIE: Oh, dear. Well there are plus points to being the only one.

MORAG: Geoffrey says like what?

BRIDIE: Like getting all the attention.

MARK: What does Geoffrey say to that?

MORAG: Nothing. I think he's sulking.

BRIDIE: Do we have to turn off at any point, darling? (*MORAG is beating up Geoffrey.*)

MARK: Not for ages yet. Morag!

MORAG: It's Geoffrey, he's being very very naughty.

BRIDIE: Geoffrey, behave! Do you want me to follow the map?

MARK: Don't worry. I've set my internal radar. I walked from Warsaw to London without a map, I think I can manage this journey.

MORAG: How did you do it, Dad? Tell us again. How did you walk all that way?

MARK: When the Germans invaded Poland my Papa said 'Go west'. Follow the sun.

BRIDIE: Daddy wasn't much older than you when he had to leave Poland and he was all on his own.

MARK: I was your age when the war started, I was fifteen by the time I reached England. How many years is that, Morag?

MORAG: Err…?

MARK: I was caught, I ran away. I was caught, I ran away again…

MORAG: Like my hamster.

MARK: (*Sings.*) Like a rubber ball I come bouncing back to you, rubber ball I come bouncing back to you, rubber ball…

MORAG: What did you eat?

MARK: Sorry?

MORAG: When you were doing all that walking. What did you eat?

MARK: Papa gave me a tin of sardines…

MORAG: Eugh!

MARK: That's all I had when I left Warsaw. By the time I reached Hungary, Morag, I was very hungry! (*MARK and MORAG laugh.*)

MORAG: Hungry, hungry…

MARK: I stole eggs from farms…

MORAG: That's naughty!

BRIDIE: It is, but not when you're starving.

MARK: I stole chickens, watches. I stole the coat from a man once who was… You'll do anything, Morag, anything to survive.

MORAG: How did you know where you were?

MARK: Sun rises in the east and sets in the west.

MORAG: Sets in his vest.

MARK: Where's the sun now, Morag? Find it and you know where you are.

MORAG: There's no sun now.

MARK: Don't be stupid, there must be sun or we'd all be dead.

MORAG: There's just a lot of cloud.

MARK: Look harder.

MORAG: There's no sun ahead of us…

MARK: No.

MORAG: Or to the side…

MARK: No. So where is it?

MORAG: On holiday?

MARK: Morag, it's behind us. That's south, so we're going?

MORAG: West?

MARK: No! I've told you this before, remember? Twelve o'clock is north.

MORAG: Oh, yes.

MARK: Three o'clock is?

MORAG: East. Six o'clock is south and nine o'clock is west.

MARK: Correct. So we are heading?

MORAG: But which way is the clock facing?

MARK: Don't they teach her anything at that school of hers, Bridie?

MORAG: I'm not very good at telling the time.

BRIDIE: She's only eight.

MORAG: I can do joined up writing and I'm milk monitor; I won a prize for my butterfly picture. Mrs Bradshaw said it was the most beautiful picture she'd ever seen, but I'm not very good at telling the time. I know my two times table and sort of know my threes. Once three is three; two threes are six; three… (*She continues.*)

BRIDIE: Tomato anyone?

MARK: Yes, please.

MORAG: Four threes are sixteen; five threes are forty.

BRIDIE: Morag? Are you going to stick those stamps in?

MORAG: Six threes are seventy-three. Seven threes are ninety…

BRIDIE: Darling, do you think we could buy a new hoover?

MARK: Not right now!

BRIDIE: It's just that mine's broken…

MORAG: Mum, I feel sick.

MARK: Oh, no!

BRIDIE: You know she gets car sick, dear. I'll open the window. (*She does so.*) It's called a Hover-Hoover. It's round and it floats. It's terribly modern.

MARK: Do you know what car sickness is, Morag?

MORAG: Horrid.

MARK: We're stationary inside the car and yet the brain knows that we're travelling. 'How can we be standing still and moving at the same time?' thinks the brain, so it gets all confused and then you feel sick.

MORAG: All the stamps are blowing everywhere!

BRIDIE: Morag!

MORAG: It's not me. It's the window. Can we stop for a bit?

MARK: We've only just started.

MORAG: I'm going to be sick!

MARK: Take your mind off it!

Singing raucously:

One man went to mow, went to mow a meadow, one man and his dog…

MORAG: Spot!

MARK: Went to mow a meadow!

MARK / MORAG: Two men went to mow, went to mow a meadow, Two men, one man, and his dog,

MORAG: Spot!

MARK / MORAG: Went to mow a meadow!

The singing gets more riotous.

BRIDIE: (*At the same time as the singing.*) Mark, Mark, keep an eye on the road. Morag, you'll make yourself sick! Mark!… Mark! I'm going to have to shut the window… I thinks that's quite enough now, you two. Morag! Alright now!

MORAG: Traffic lights! (*They stop singing.*)

Pause.

Amber…green. Isn't the amber light beautiful? Am-ber. Oh I wish I'd brought my bead box with me. I didn't think I'd need it.

BRIDIE: You never know, do you?

MORAG: I've got some amber beads in it.

MARK: They're not amber, they're plastic.

MORAG: No they're not. They're the same as Mum's.

BRIDIE: They look the same, like your diamonds look the same, but there's a big difference. If you look carefully at my amber beads there's a fly in one of them.

MORAG: I know, it's horrid.

BRIDIE: Well that shows that it's real amber.

MORAG: How long has it been trapped in there?

BRIDIE: Since prehistoric times.

MARK: Prehysterical times.

MORAG: I hope it doesn't get out.

BRIDIE: Why dear?

MORAG: It'll be very angry. (*MARK and BRIDIE laugh.*)

MARK: Put wood under pressure you get coal, put coal under pressure you get diamonds.

MORAG: There's an AA Man. Salute! (*They all salute.*)

BRIDIE: It looks really good, the Hover-Hoover. I saw an advertisement on ITV.

MARK: I've told you before, that channel's rubbish.

BRIDIE: I know, I tuned into it accidently.

MARK: Be more careful!

MORAG: What's wrong with ITV, Mum?

BRIDIE: It's common.

MORAG: Oh.

MARK: If you hadn't been watching ITV, you wouldn't know about the Hover-Hoover. Commercials!

MORAG: Can we stop if we see a milk machine?

BRIDIE: Here, darling, have a lovely tomato.

MORAG: Can we go on a hovercraft, dad?

MARK: We'll see.

MORAG: Do they fly above the water?

MARK: No. They ride on a cushion of high pressure air, free from all contact with the surface beneath.

BRIDIE: Are they safe?

MARK: Of course they're safe. They'd hardly bring them into service if they weren't safe.

MORAG: Oh, there's a milk machine!

BRIDIE: We'll stop at the next one, darling.

MARK: They're a British invention you know, Morag, hovercrafts. Cockerell is the name of the chappy who invented them.

MORAG: Really?

MARK: Yes. But he doesn't like to crow about it. (*He laughs.*)

MORAG: That's not true.

MARK: It is.

MORAG: That's not his real name.

MARK: It is.
Cock-a-doodle do,
The dame has lost her shoe,
The master's lost his fiddling stick,
And doesn't know what to do.

MORAG: Will you take us on a hovercraft?

BRIDIE: Shall I pop along to Whiteleys and put a deposit down on the Hoover?

MORAG: I want to go on a hovercraft. I want to go on a hovercraft!

MARK: I want! I want! I want doesn't get!

MORAG: Why not?

MARK: I'm taking you for a nice drive but it's not enough is it?

BRIDIE: Oh, that's not true, Mark, we do appreciate it.

MARK: No you don't. You expect it. As you expect everything else that arrives by magic carpet: food, clothes, money. (*Singing.*) Oh, yes, I'm the great provider!

BRIDIE: Oh, Mark, don't be a pig!

MARK: Sorry?

BRIDIE: We were only talking…

MARK: I am not the pig. I am not the pig!

BRIDIE: All right now…

MARK: You two are the pigs.

BRIDIE: Mark!

MARK: You just called me one! You two are like cuckoos, for ever sitting there with your mouths open. I'm sorry but greed is the word that comes to mind, Bridie, and it's an ugly word, an ugly word. What happens when you're greedy, Morag? Morag, you know.

MORAG: You get fat.

MARK: That's right and are fat people pretty or ugly?

MORAG: Ugly.

MARK: And do you want to be an ugly person?

MORAG: No.

MARK: Right. So stop being greedy and Bridie, I think we should try and think of others less fortunate than ourselves. Agreed?

BRIDIE: Agreed.

MARK: (*Singing.*)
Oh, would you like to swing on a star,
Carry moon beams home in a jar?
You'd be better off than you are,
Or would you rather be a pig?

Come on Morag, you're not singing! (*MORAG joins in weakly.*)

A pig is an animal with dirt on its face,
A pig is a terrible disgrace.
He's got no manners when he eats his food,
He's fat and dirty and extremely rude.
So if you don't give a feather or a fig,
You might grow up to be a pig.

MARK takes out his mouth organ from his jacket pocket and plays it while driving.

MORAG: It's getting dark. I can't see out the window properly.

BRIDIE: Play with Geoffrey then.

MORAG: I can't. He's ill. He has to have complete rest. Actually I think he might have to have an operation.

BRIDIE: What for?

MORAG: He's got heart problems.

BRIDIE: How can you tell?

MORAG: He looks very pale. I think he's going to die. If he dies will he go to heaven?

BRIDIE: If he's been a good rabbit.

MORAG: Oh, no. (*Pause.*) All I can see is the lights of the other cars coming towards us and black.

MARK: Let's have the radio on. (*Cilla Black comes on singing 'You're my world'.*)

MORAG: (*Over the intro.*) Oh, no. (*She collapses on the seat.*)

BRIDIE: Who's this?

MORAG: It's Cilla. (*They listen to the opening few lines.*)

BRIDIE: She's very good isn't she? Is she?

MORAG: Yuk!

BRIDIE: She's going to do the Royal Command Performance.

MARK: I can't hear.

MORAG: She was on Pinky and Perky last week. (*They listen.*)

BRIDIE: She's getting married to that nice man, what's his name?

MORAG: Ken Dodd.

BRIDIE: Don't be silly.

MORAG: If Cilla married Ken Dodd she'd be Cilla Dodd.

BRIDIE: Bobby, that's it

MORAG: (*Laughing.*) Cilla Dodd.

BRIDIE: (*Imitating a scouse accent.*) My Bobby. My Bobby.

MARK: Shut up!

BRIDIE: Sorry.

> *We listen to some more. When she gets to 'with your hand, resting in mine…' MORAG joins in.*

MORAG: I hate it when she does that. (*MORAG imitates her.*) She's stupid.

BRIDIE: I think she's very nice.

MORAG: She's a friend of the Beatles.

BRIDIE: I don't think so.

MORAG: Yes she is.

BRIDIE: You're thinking of that barefoot one, what's her name?

MORAG: Sandy Shaw.

BRIDIE: You'd think she'd put her shoes on wouldn't you?

MORAG: No, Cilla knows the Beatles.

MARK: Will you two bloody shut up! (*They listen to a bit more.*)

BRIDIE: He's a hairdresser, you know.

MORAG: Who?

BRIDIE: Her fiancé.

MORAG: No he's not.

MARK: Right, that's it. (*MARK stops the car and the radio.*)

MORAG: What? (*MARK exits.*) Dad!

BRIDIE: Don't be long, dear.

MORAG: Where's he going?

BRIDIE: For a walk.

MORAG: Let's go too.

BRIDIE: I think he needs a little break.

MORAG: Oh, what have we done?

BRIDIE: We haven't done anything. Let's stay here and have a nice time.

MORAG: Turn the radio back on, Mum.

BRIDIE: It doesn't work when the car's not going.

MORAG: Ohhh! (*Pause.*) Is he going to get me my milk?

BRIDIE: I'm sure he will. I'm sure he will.

MORAG: It's raining, it's pouring, the old man's snoring,
He went to bed and bumped his head
And couldn't get up in the morning.

(*Pointing to raindrops on her window.*) This raindrop's me and that raindrop's Geoffrey. They're getting bigger, they're filling up, which one is going to roll first? I'm off! And here comes Geoffrey's. No chance, Geoffrey. I'm the winner!

BRIDIE: We should be more careful. He loves a drive, it's his way of relaxing.

MORAG: Two more. Neck and neck…

BRIDIE: I'm no sailor, but I love to crew.

MORAG: I win again. Sorry, Geoffrey. (*Pause.*) Is he coming yet?

BRIDIE: Not yet, dear. He does get tired. We should remember that he works very hard; we should try and think about him a bit more.

MORAG: I'm always thinking about him. You always take his side.

BRIDIE: You and I talk a lot and Daddy finds it difficult especially when he's trying to listen to the radio. (*MORAG pretends she's dying dramatically.*) I'm not taking sides, I'm trying to understand his point of view. You see sometimes, darling… Why's that woman staring at us? You see, Morag… (*BRIDIE turns and sees MORAG.*) Stop that! Morag, stop it! (*BRIDIE, embarrassed, smiles at the onlooker.*)

MORAG: The woman's laughing!

BRIDIE: You mustn't do things like that!

MORAG: Why not?

BRIDIE: It's just not done. (*Pause.*)

MORAG: Let's go for our own walk.

BRIDIE: We're looking after the car.

MORAG: Just a little one.

BRIDIE: What if Dad comes back and finds us gone?

MORAG: Good.

BRIDIE: Morag!

MORAG: Maybe he's dropped out.

BRIDIE: Dad, would never drop out.

MORAG: Why not?

BRIDIE: Because he's not like that.

MORAG: Mum, what's a drop out?

BRIDIE: Someone who drops out.

MORAG: But what do they drop out of?

BRIDIE: Life.

MORAG: Are they dead then?

BRIDIE: No, they drop out of their own life.

MORAG: Is there a heap of them somewhere? Where do they go?

BRIDIE: They don't go anywhere.

MORAG: Are they dangerous?

BRIDIE: Well, yes in a way, they are.

MORAG: Why?

BRIDIE: If we all dropped out, everything would stop.

MORAG: That would be terrible.

BRIDIE: Terrible. (*Pause.*)

MORAG: What do they look like?

BRIDIE: Scruffy, usually, with long hair and sandals…

MORAG: Like Jesus?

BRIDIE: No. Not like Jesus. Like... like the Rolling Stones. (*Pause.*)

MORAG: Maybe he's never coming back.

BRIDIE: Don't be silly!

MORAG: No, really. Maybe he's gone for ever and we're going to have to look after ourselves. We'd have to sleep in the car.

BRIDIE: I don't think so, darling.

MORAG: We'd have to beg for money and people would walk past us because we smell and our clothes would turn to rags and we would have to get our food from people's dustbins...

BRIDIE: I think I see him coming.

MORAG: We could live on wild berries but then we'd eat something poisonous and be ill...

BRIDIE: Oh, maybe not.

MORAG: And the doctor wouldn't know where to find us and we'd rot and dogs would eat us because they wouldn't know we're supposed to be people. (*Pause.*) Mum, do dogs eat people?

BRIDIE: No darling.

MORAG: But they would, wouldn't they, if they didn't know it was a person?

BRIDIE: Why don't you have a little sleep?

MORAG: I wonder what we taste like? (*MORAG chews her hand.*)

BRIDIE: Let's sit here quietly for a while and have a little rest.

MORAG: I wonder if we all taste different? Like different

fish. I wonder if Granny's dog would eat people?

BRIDIE: I'm going to have a nice quiet time now. You too darling.

MORAG: (*Pause.*) I try to stop talking but I can't. If you could drive we could drive off now.

BRIDIE: And leave Daddy? Poor Daddy.

MORAG: Yeah, go on, Mum, turn the car on. Turn it on. Let's go, let's go!

BRIDIE: Stop it! Here he comes!

MORAG: Here's Daddy! Hurray! Here he comes, Mum!

Enter MARK.

MARK: (*Singing.*) It's only me from over the sea…

MORAG: Says Barnacle Bill the Sailor

MARK: All dressed up like a Christmas tree.

MORAG: Says Barnacle Bill the Sailor!

MARK: Crew all ship shape?

MORAG: Aye, aye, Captain. (*MORAG salutes.*)

MARK: Anchors away! (*He starts the car.*)
(*Singing.*) In the town where I was born, lived a man who sailed to sea,

MORAG joins in:
And he told us of his life, in the land of submarines.
So we sailed unto the sun till we found the sea of green,
And we lived beneath the waves in our yellow submarine.
We all live in a yellow submarine, yellow submarine, yellow submarine.

MARK plays along with his mouth organ.

We all live in a yellow submarine, yellow submarine, yellow submarine.

MORAG: (*Hand over her mouth making sea noises and saying:*) Full speed ahead, Mr Father, full speed ahead.

MARK: We're under the water now. This is a special submarine car. There's a huge pink octopus.

MORAG: He's waving. (*She waves back.*)

MARK: There's millions of tiny rainbow fish. All moving together. They've never seen a sea-car before.

MORAG: I'm a water baby. I can stay under water for ever if I like, my long hair floats out behind me waving like sea weed.

MARK: I'm a deep sea diver, and I have dived deeper than any man has ever dived before, my friends are the big ugly fishes of the deep.

MORAG: Who are you, Mum?

BRIDIE: Oh, I'm a mermaid. I sit on a rock and I comb my long beautiful hair.

MORAG: No, you've got to be under water.

BRIDIE: I can go under water if I like or I can sit on my rock if I like.

MORAG: I collect star fish.

MARK: I go looking for treasure in beautiful boxes that lie almost buried at the bottom of the sea. Little treasure chests and when you open them they're full of sparkling gold coins.

BRIDIE: I am a siren.

MORAG: (*Makes the noise of a police car.*) Ner-ner-ner-ner.

BRIDIE: No, not that kind of siren, I beckon sailors to their death.

MORAG: Eurgh!

MARK: What sits on the bottom of the sea and shakes?

MORAG: I don't know, Dad, what sits on the bottom of the sea and shakes?

MARK: A nervous wreck!

MORAG: Good one!

BRIDIE: I get it! (*MORAG puts her arms around her mother.*)

MORAG: Well done, Mum! Isn't this great? All being out together, this is the best drive we've ever had, isn't it, Dad? (*MORAG puts her arms around her father.*)

MARK: Morag! That is so dangerous, you don't know how dangerous that is!

MORAG: (*Pause.*) I'm always talking to the back of your head.

MARK: So?

MORAG: It's like you're there, right, and I'm here, right, and I can only see your eyes in the mirror.

MARK: I can see you fine. Bridie, did you catch that last road sign?

BRIDIE: No, I wasn't really looking.

MARK: Oh, it's turning off time soon.

BRIDIE: Oh, right. Would you like me to look at the map?

MARK: If you would.

MORAG: Look, Dad, there's a man up ahead with a big red sign with "stop" on it!

BRIDIE: What is it? What's the matter?

MARK: It's all right. It's just some country bumpkin with his cows. How long are we going to be stuck behind this lot? Oh, sod it! (*MARK leans out of the car window.*) Hurry up, will you, for God's sake! Move your fat arses!

MORAG: Mark!

MARK: (*Out the window.*) Same to you with brass knobs on!

BRIDIE: They're going as fast as they can.

MORAG: Why are they walking on the road?

BRIDIE: The farmer's taking them for milking.

MORAG: Ask him for some milk for me.

BRIDIE: No. You can't.

MORAG: Why not?

MARK: (*They start moving again.*) Oh, thank God for that.

MORAG: Why didn't you ask him for my milk?

BRIDIE: It's not safe when it comes straight from the cow, it's full of disease.

MORAG: Honest?

BRIDIE: Yes. It's got to be boiled before you can drink it.

MORAG: Eugh! Full of disease!

MARK: It has to be pasteurised.

BRIDIE: That's right. Where are we now, dear?

MARK: You've got the map. Louis Pasteur, Morag? The man in the big portrait at my lab. He founded the Institut Pasteur in Paris in 1888, and pioneered pasteurisation.

MORAG: I'm never drinking milk again!

MARK: It's not actually boiled, Bridie, because that would affect the taste.

BRIDIE: Oh, I'm not very good at this, I can never work out which way to turn the map.

MARK: Turn it in the direction we're travelling.

BRIDIE: Right.

MARK: He also developed the vaccine for rabies, Morag.

MORAG: Oh.

BRIDIE: Right, I've got London, but that's not much use is it, that was ages ago.

MARK: Leave it Bridie. Monkey, what did that sign say?

MORAG: I can't read big words.

MARK: Oh, God!

BRIDIE: Are we lost?

MARK: Don't be ridiculous!

MORAG: We've just passed a sign with a big 'P' on it

MARK: What?

MORAG: A big letter 'P' on it and there's another one with a picture of a phone on it.

MARK: OK. I'm fine now, thank you, you two.

BRIDIE: Are you sure, dear?

MARK: Yep. Just fine.

BRIDIE: Look at all that muck on the windscreen, tut… (*BRIDIE wipes the windscreen with her tissue.*)

MARK: Use the shammy. (*She does.*)

BRIDIE: It's on the outside.

MARK: What?

BRIDIE: Those smears, what are they?

MORAG: They're dead insects, hit by the car at a million miles an hour and… Splat!

MARK: That's enough, Morag!

BRIDIE: We won't be able to see out properly.

MARK: I can see fine.

MORAG: They'll be all over the head lights as well.

Squashed! Don't be afraid of the spider, Geoffrey, look at the size of him and look at the size of you! (*MORAG squashes Geoffrey who dies a painful and vocal death.*)

MARK: What are you doing, Morag?

BRIDIE: Can we slow down a little darling?

MARK: We're only doing fifty!

BRIDIE: Is that all?

MORAG: Little things get squashed…

BRIDIE: Slow down a bit anyway.

MARK: We have to make up time.

MORAG: By bigger things. (*She continues to beat up Geoffrey.*)

BRIDIE: We'll have to stop!

MARK: Why?

BRIDIE: I'll have to clean the windscreen!

MARK: It's fine!

    MORAG is still murdering Geoffrey.

    Morag!!

BRIDIE: There is no point in arriving filthy dirty. No point in arriving at all.

MARK: I'm not telling you again, Morag!

MORAG: It's not me, it's Geoffrey! (*Dad stops the car. Gets out, opens MORAG's door.*) I'm sorry, Daddy, I didn't mean to, I'm sorry…

MARK: You stupid little… (*MARK hits MORAG.*)

MORAG: Don't!

BRIDIE: Mark, it's all right!

MARK: It's not all right! It's not bloody all right at all!

(MARK gets back in the car and starts up again. MORAG is sobbing gently.)

MORAG: I'm sorry.

BRIDIE: You're a big girl now and you'll have to stop playing those silly games.

MORAG: It wasn't me…

MARK: Morag!

MORAG: Sorry.

MARK: Ah, Kendal, good, we're on the right road.

BRIDIE: Good. *(Pause.)*

MARK: Have you heard of Kendal Mint Cake, Morag? *(MORAG mumbles something.)* I can't hear you.

MORAG: No.

MARK: Would you like to know what it is?

BRIDIE: It's very sugary and very minty.

MARK: That's right. Climbers use it for extra energy. But it's not a cake it's a bar of compressed sugar and peppermint. There are lots of mountains around here and when the climbing gets tough they have a little bit of Kendal Mint Cake and it gives them a lift.

MORAG: Can we get some?

MARK: The shops are all shut now. Another time, maybe. Kendall? Wasn't that the name of the American chappy who won the Nobel Prize for medicine?

BRIDIE: Was it, dear?

MARK: Yes. 1950. He shared it with someone that year… Who was it now?

BRIDIE: I can't think.

MARK: Work on the adrenal gland. Very important work and he was acknowledged for it.

BRIDIE: Is it true that Alfred Nobel made his money from explosives?

MARK: Go on.

BRIDIE: I read it in your *Time Magazine.*

MARK: He also invented ballistite. He made his fortune from the manufacture of explosives which of course he put in trust for the Nobel Prize fund.

BRIDIE: Isn't it ironic that that money is used for the Nobel Peace Prize?

MARK: Why?

BRIDIE: I'm just saying…

MARK: Where would we be without defence? You sound like one of those beatniks who use award ceremonies to rant on against Vietnam.

BRIDIE: For God's sake…

MARK: For God's sake what, Bridie?

BRIDIE: I was only making conversation.

MARK: No. You brought up the subject of arms and some left-wing propaganda and I'd like to hear more of what you think. Go on.

BRIDIE: About what?

MARK: About the sale of arms and explosives. What do you think?

BRIDIE: Ideally it would be wonderful to live in a world that didn't need those things.

MARK: Go on.

BRIDIE: But we do need them.

MARK: That's right. And Nobel? What kind of a man was he?

BRIDIE: I've no idea.

MARK: Oh, I thought you were a bit of an authority on the subject.

BRIDIE: Mark…

MARK: What?

BRIDIE: You're being horrid.

MARK: I'm pointing out to you how foolish you can appear when you talk about a subject you know nothing about.

BRIDIE: Okay.

MARK: Nothing! You know nothing about it but it doesn't stop you having an opinion, does it? Facts picked up from magazines and ITV. And hey presto, you're a world authority.

BRIDIE: Stop it!

MARK: Sorry?

BRIDIE: Stop it! Stop it! Stop it! Morag and I we can't say anything, we can't do anything! I can't stand it!

MARK: Really. (*MARK stops the car.*)

BRIDIE: What are you doing? I'm sorry.

MARK: No.

BRIDIE: No really. We're all a little tired. If we have a little sleep everything will be better.

MARK: I don't think so, Bridie. (*He gets out.*)

BRIDIE: Mark! Get back in the car! (*MARK walks away.*) Mark!

MORAG: Daddy!

MARK: What can I do, Monkey, what can I do? (*Exit MARK.*)

MORAG: What have you done?

BRIDIE: Stupid idiot.

MORAG: He's not! He's not!

BRIDIE: No, I know he's not, darling, but sometimes he gets me so angry.

MORAG: Call him back.

BRIDIE: He'll be back, darling, you know what he's like. He just needs a…

MORAG: Dad!

BRIDIE: Morag!

MORAG: Dad!

BRIDIE: Stop it, Morag. It's all right. Come in the front with me, pet.

MORAG: No.

BRIDIE: Where's Geoffrey?

MORAG: He's dead.

BRIDIE: Oh, dear.

MORAG: His heart burst. Ages ago. And nobody noticed.

BRIDIE: Oh, dear. Let me see if I can't make him better.

MORAG: You can't make him better, don't be stupid. He's dead I told you!

BRIDIE: Alright, dear. (*Pause.*) We'll never get anywhere if he keeps doing this.

MORAG: He hates us.

BRIDIE: No he doesn't.

MORAG: Yes he does and he's gone and he's never coming back and it's all your fault and I hate you and you are the pig, the big fat pig!

MORAG climbs into the driving seat.

BRIDIE: What are you doing?

MORAG: I'm going to drive after him. (*She turns on the ignition and turns the wheel, as children do when they're playing at driving.*)

BRIDIE: Stop it!

MORAG: He's not coming back, thicky! It's not going, it's not going, do something!

BRIDIE: It's the pedals, you can't reach the pedals.

MORAG: I can, I can. Oh, Mum! Mum! Mum! (*MORAG starts to cry.*)

BRIDIE: Come here, pet. Shhhh... Shhhh...

MORAG: What are we going to do, Mum?

BRIDIE: I don't know, pet. (*Pause.*)

MORAG: Are we having a quiet time?

BRIDIE: I'm thinking.

MORAG: I'll never leave you, Mum.

BRIDIE: Alright, darling.

MORAG: Geoffrey's not really dead.

BRIDIE: I know. Let's bring him in the front with us.

MORAG: Come on, Geoffrey. He says that he's going to sit in the window and be the guard.

BRIDIE: Good. (*Pause.*) Are you all right?

MORAG: Yeah. Are you all right?

BRIDIE: Yeah. (*Pause.*)

MORAG: Where are we, Mum?

BRIDIE: I've no idea, darling, no idea.

Lights fade to black.

ACT TWO

1972. The car is turned side-on to the audience. There are gingham curtains on the windows, tied back with ribbons and an awning supported on poles. A small table with wet wrung washing on it, a pile of fire wood and two tin buckets, one empty and one with water and potatoes in.

BRIDIE is sitting alone calmly washing the last of the spuds and putting them in a pot. She wipes her hands on her apron, picks up the empty bucket and exits.

MORAG enters, wildly riding a pretend horse.

MORAG: Eeee-haaa! We've shaken them off, Trigger! We're a team you and me. (*She dismounts and pretends to spit.*) Oh, yes, indeedy. They'll never find us here, we can rest for a while and when we're ready, we'll saddle up and ride on. (*She scratches her head vigorously.*) O-oh, looks like spuds again for tea! It's alright for you Trigger, you eat grass, you like grass, you don't mind that there's nothing but grass. But for us humans it's different. We like a change, occasionally. Tonight I would like fish fingers, ten of them, two whole hands of fish fingers with a bit of… (*There is a noise off.*) Someone's coming. Quick, scatter.

She hides. Enter BRIDIE carrying a bucket of water.

Stick 'em up!

BRIDIE screams.

BRIDIE: Morag!

MORAG: (*Laughing.*) Got you!

BRIDIE: You scared the living daylights out of me! (*MORAG laughs.*) You're home early.

MORAG: Yeah, last lesson was singing and Jenny and I got bored so we bunked off. (*Singing dramatically.*) "Who are the yeomen, the yeomen of England? Dee dee dee dum, dee dee dee dum, dee dee dee dum!" We decided we didn't care so we left.

BRIDIE: Oh, no.

MORAG: No one noticed.

BRIDIE: You'll get in trouble.

MORAG: No one noticed.

BRIDIE: The Head'll call me in again.

MORAG: There was a riot in the class, there always is with Miss Felsham. She won't have seen us go. (*MORAG scratches her hair again.*)

BRIDIE: Hmm. Here, I've left you some water to wash your hair.

MORAG: I'm not using that, it's filthy!

BRIDIE: And so's your hair. I've made some nice nettle shampoo. Come on. (*BRIDIE physically bends MORAG to the bucket.*)

MORAG: Get off. I don't need to wash it!

BRIDIE: You're tearing at it.

MORAG: It doesn't matter. I'll do it in a minute. (*She goes and looks at the traffic, the audience.*) Wow! That's what I call a jam!

BRIDIE: Come away from there.

MORAG: I thought it was building up, Mum, oh, yes! There's a new Ford Granada over there and steam's coming out of it, come and look. (*BRIDIE joins her.*) Look, they're pushing it to the side.

BRIDIE: Something must have happened miles away and this is the tail back. (*MORAG scratches her head.*) Come on, we don't want them to see us.

MORAG: It doesn't matter if people see us. Look there's an AA man arriving, he'll sort it. (*She salutes. BRIDIE goes back to the car.*) People don't salute them any more. Mum, how old do you have to be before you can have driving lessons?

BRIDIE: I don't know, sixteen, seventeen.

MORAG: That's for ever!

BRIDIE: No it's not. It's only four years. Four years can pass in a trice.

MORAG: Are we going to be here for another four years?

BRIDIE: I don't know, sweetheart. Will you give me a hand with this washing?

MORAG: Yeah. (*Not moving.*) I'm going to buy a Jag when I can drive.

BRIDIE: Oh, yes?

MORAG: A red Mark 2, with a silver leaping Jaguar on the front.

BRIDIE: You'll have to have a good job.

MORAG: I'm going to be an engineer.

BRIDIE: I thought you were going to be a vet?

MORAG: No. Perhaps I'll be an AA Man. (*MORAG salutes.*) Aye, aye, captain. Yeah, I'll ride up to people in my uniform. (*In her cowboy voice.*): "Ma'm, what seems to be the trouble? Oh, I'll have that sorted in no time." (*She salutes three times.*) Yes-Sir-eee. (*She sings. Saluting on each sea/see.*)

A sailor went to sea, sea, sea,
To see what he could see, see, see.
But all that he could see, see, see,
Was the bottom of the deep blue sea, sea, sea.

Pause.

BRIDIE: Come here, darling, pass me the pegs.

MORAG: I'm going to be an engineer like Brunel. Isambard Kingdom Brunel. We're doing him in history, he's fantastic! I'm going to build bridges, huge bridges. (*She goes to BRIDIE.*) He built a massive bridge in Bristol and he built tunnels with his Dad. And guess what his Dad's name was.

BRIDIE: I've no idea.

MORAG: Mark!

BRIDIE: Really?

MORAG: Yeah, the same as Daddy.

BRIDIE: You'll have to work hard at school if you want to be an engineer. (*Pause.*)

MORAG: I don't know why you're so funny about people seeing us. (*Pause.*) No one's told us off.

BRIDIE: Leave it now, Morag.

MORAG: It's really hard not telling people.

BRIDIE: Not telling people what?

MORAG: (*Shouting.*) Where we live!

BRIDIE: Look, you tell them we live at the farm!

MORAG: I do, but…

BRIDIE: So, what's the problem?

MORAG: We don't really live on the farm.

BRIDIE: Morag, people would look down on us if they knew where we lived. Now peel those potatoes. (*MORAG half-heartedly goes to the potatoes.*)

MORAG: I wanted to ask Jenny over.

BRIDIE: Have you told Jenny where we live?

MORAG: No!

BRIDIE: Have you?

MORAG: No! But she's my best friend, I don't like having secrets.

BRIDIE: You can't tell everyone everything.

MORAG: She thinks I don't like her 'cos I never bring her back here.

BRIDIE: Look, we live here without Daddy…

MORAG: So?

BRIDIE: I don't want people knowing. It's not…safe.

MORAG: I think you should be proud of us. We cope without a man. We're Women's Lib. (*MORAG very slowly starts to peel the potatoes.*)

BRIDIE: I am proud of us.

MORAG: No you're not. You hide.

BRIDIE: We're not hiding…

MORAG: We're like two frightened rabbits.

BRIDIE: We keep ourselves to ourselves…

MORAG: We're like weirdos. We're going to be here in fifty years' time, all on our own. Two old ladies, peeling spuds and creeping around.

They start speaking together:

BRIDIE: Morag!

MORAG: Smelly and in rags and people will think that we're witches…

BRIDIE: I'm not listening.

MORAG: …and horrid little boys will throw stones at us and call us names. Haggy-hags! Creepy hags! Weirdos!

BRIDIE: Stop it, Morag!

MORAG: And one day they'll drag us screaming to the river and push us in. Help! Help! Help! we'll scream. And well drown and nobody'll care. They'll all be dancing and singing: My ding-a-ling, my ding-a-ling. I want you to play with my ding-a-ling!

BRIDIE: Morag!

MORAG: (*Manic.*) My ding-a-ling, my ding-a-ling, I want you to play with my ding-a-ling!

BRIDIE: (*Shaking MORAG.*) Stop it! Stop it! Stop it! (*Pause.*)

MORAG: Anyway, Jenny's coming over next Wednesday.

BRIDIE: Sorry?

MORAG: I've asked her…

BRIDIE: No.

MORAG: And she's coming…

BRIDIE: She bloody isn't!

MORAG: You hate my friends! (*MORAG runs and hides in the car.*)

BRIDIE: Oh, Morag! Please, darling. I've had a long day, I'm tired. (*BRIDIE waits for a response.*) Let's talk about this later. (*No response.*) Morag, it's not that I hate your friends. (*No response.*) I didn't want to tell you this, Morag, but there's been a man… A man, hanging around. (*No response.*) There's nothing to be frightened of but I've…

MORAG: (*From the car.*) You're just saying that.

BRIDIE: No, honestly, I heard footsteps last night.

MORAG: (*Getting out of the car.*) So?

BRIDIE: I caught a glimpse of him, today. Just his back. He had a tweed jacket on… I don't know… So, I want us to keep our heads down. Do you understand?

MORAG shrugs her shoulders. BRIDIE gets on with the dinner. MORAG ambles about.

Haven't you any homework to be getting on with?

MORAG: Nope.

BRIDIE: You must have.

MORAG: I'm still on that stupid nature project and I'm stuck –

BRIDIE: Why don't you get it and let's see if we can't unstick you.

MORAG: (*She gets her books from her bag.*) I'm not frightened.

BRIDIE: That's good, dear.

MOAG: I'm not, really.

BRIDIE: Good. So what's the problem with it?

MORAG: It's rubbish!

BRIDIE: Oh, Morag, don't say that. All you've got to do is collect bits of nature.

MORAG: No. It's "Nature Through the Seasons" and it's stupid 'cos it's spring so we can only collect things from spring. Jenny's put a squashed fly in hers, with an arrow pointing to it saying: Fly. (*MORAG laughs, BRIDIE raises her eyebrows.*) It's nature! It's only a joke but Mr Walsh is going to do his nut. I hate him. (*Pause.*) Mum, can girls be engineers?

BRIDIE: I suppose so. Girls can be anything nowadays.

MORAG: Tell Mr Walsh. When I asked him for some names of women engineers he just laughed.

BRIDIE: Did he now?

MORAG: He said he couldn't think of any.

BRIDIE: You'll have to be the first, then. (*MORAG grins.*) Those pressed buttercups have come out well… I haven't seen this drawing before. (*MORAG pulls a face.*) What kind of bird is it?

MORAG: It's a tit.

BRIDIE: Lovely.

MORAG: (*She laughs.*) A great tit. A great titty.

BRIDIE: Alright, darling. You should write its name underneath.

MORAG: Hmm… Maybe I'll turn it into a sparrow.

BRIDIE: And is she sitting on her nest?

MORAG: Yeah.

BRIDIE: Well that's nice and spring-like… And what's that black blobby bit next to her?

MORAG: That's one of her chicks. She's sitting on them.

BRIDIE: I don't think mother birds sit on their chicks. They sit on their eggs… Yes… But not on their…

MORAG: (*Taking the project.*) I told you it was rubbish.

BRIDIE: It's not. Come on now. (*Takes project back.*) What are these blank white pages?

MORAG: They're winter. That's all the snow.

BRIDIE: Oh.

MORAG: Only joking! Those are pages for summer and I can't do them.

BRIDIE: Well what are summery things?

MORAG: I don't know… (*MORAG starts scratching her hair.*)

BRIDIE: What about the sun?

MORAG: Yeah…

BRIDIE: And?

MORAG: I think we should get a gun.

BRIDIE: Sorry?

MORAG: To protect ourselves. I think we should get a great long shotgun, like you see in the movies.

BRIDIE: No, I don't…

MORAG: Why not? We're sitting targets here. We wouldn't get in trouble, not if we used it in self-defence, I'm sure. We wouldn't go to jail or anything. (*She acts out the following.*) We'd warn them of course and if they still came towards us, we'd blow their brains out!

BRIDIE: I don't think it's that simple.

MORAG: We should get one and practise, so we're ready. We can use old baked-bean cans, a row of them on top of the car and then pick them off one by one. (*She does so, then blows on the ends of her fingers.*)

BRIDIE: Come here, dear, let's finish your homework.

MORAG: (*In cowboy voice.*) There could be trouble tonight!

BRIDIE: (*Reading the project.*) Hmm?

MORAG: One-Eyed Jake's in town.

BRIDIE: Oh, yeah?

MORAG: I've been looking forward to him paying a visit. Oh, yes, indeedy!

BRIDIE: (*Reading.*) But he's the most wanted bank robber in the west.

MORAG: (*Breaking out of the fantasy.*) Mum! He's not a bank robber, he's a cattle rustler!

BRIDIE: Sorry, darling.

MORAG: Black Pete is the bank robber.

BRIDIE: I get them all confused.

MORAG: Well don't.

BRIDIE: Come here. (*MORAG goes to BRIDIE.*) All you have to do…

MORAG: Ohhhh! (*She scratches her head vigorously.*)

BRIDIE: Is draw some icicles…

MORAG: I don't wanna do it.

BRIDIE: (*MORAG is still scratching her head.*) Stop scratching your… (*BRIDIE stares down at the book.*) What are those?

MORAG: What?

BRIDIE: Shake your head again… Here, over the book.

MORAG: What are they?

BRIDIE: It's coming out of your hair!

MORAG: What? What is it?

BRIDIE: Oh, it's just bits of… It's nothing.

MORAG: Let me see. (*Grabs book and scrutinises the pages.*) They're moving! (*MORAG screams and drops book, madly dances and shakes her head and screaming.*)

BRIDIE: Morag!

MORAG: God. Get them out! Get them out!

BRIDIE: If you keep still I'll…

MORAG: What are they?

BRIDIE: Morag!! (*BRIDIE manages to contain her in her arms.*)

MORAG: (*Sobbing.*) What is it, Mama?

BRIDIE: It's alright, they're nothing, only nits.

MORAG: Nits! (*MORAG stares aghast.*)

BRIDIE: They're very common. They're little creaturey things. Let's have a look.

MORAG: No!

MORAG goes over to the bucket and plunges her hair in it. BRIDIE follows her, picks up a bar of soap and washes her hair.

BRIDIE: We'll wash them away. We'll brush them away. And then they'll be gone.

MORAG: Who gave them to me?

BRIDIE: It could be anyone, it doesn't matter.

MORAG: I'll kill them. Don't tell anybody! (*BRIDIE rinses the hair with a cup.*)

BRIDIE: Oh, well... We'll see.

MORAG: I don't want anyone to know. Don't tell anyone. Promise. I don't want to be the one with nits. I don't want to be the one with nits!

BRIDIE: Okay, darling.

MORAG: If you tell people they won't come near me!

BRIDIE: Okay. Here wrap this around your head.

BRIDIE gives MORAG a towel and goes to get a comb from the front of the car.

Come here.

BRIDIE sits in a chair and MORAG sits at her feet. BRIDIE combs ribs of MORAG's hair over and over.

MORAG: Who gave them to me?

BRIDIE: It doesn't matter. You're not frightened of a few little nits, are you?

MORAG: It's digusting.

BRIDIE: (*Picks out the lice and is disgusted.*) No it's not.

MORAG: We live here with wild things, so they think we're animals. I hate it here! I want to live in a proper house! I want to go home!

BRIDIE: Morag, please. One day you tell me you love it here, the next day you hate it.

MORAG: Well, I love it and hate it.

BRIDIE: I like being close to nature.

MORAG: There's nothing here, Mum. In London there were shops and parks and cinemas. We haven't even got a telly.

BRIDIE: So?

MORAG: But they talk about telly at school all the time and I can't join in.

BRIDIE: Then talk about something else.

MORAG: What?

BRIDIE: When I was your age we didn't have a telly. We used to talk about all sorts of things.

MORAG: Like?

BRIDIE: Like…our pets and…

MORAG: I haven't got any pets…

BRIDIE: Well alright, we used to talk about our parents and what they did and.. (*BRIDIE stops combing MORAG's hair and sits down next to her.*)

MORAG: Why doesn't he come and find us, Mum?

BRIDIE: I don't know, darling.

MORAG: What did we do wrong? (*Pause.*) I know what it was, we talked too much. (*BRIDIE smiles.*) You hate it here too, Mum.

BRIDIE: No, I don't.

MORAG: I've heard you crying at night.

BRIDIE: Sometimes I miss things from home…

MORAG: Like?

BRIDIE: Oh, like my nice china and glasses…

MORAG: And Daddy? Do you miss Daddy?

BRIDIE: Of course I do.

MORAG: I miss going to exciting places…

BRIDIE: Yes, and having more money! But I don't miss the horrid things.

MORAG: What horrid things?

BRIDIE: Well, now we can talk as much as we like and not upset anyone.

MORAG: Yeah, but we haven't anything to talk about.

BRIDIE: We do okay. (*She returns to combing MORAG's hair.*) Look at all this lovely space and birds and green…

MORAG: Yeah and nits.

BRIDIE: You didn't catch them here. You'll have caught them at school, I'm sure of that. When I was at school the nuns used to line us up and comb through our hair like this, looking really closely at our scalps but we didn't know what they were looking for. A rumour started that they were checking to see if our brains were leaking out.

MORAG: (*Laughing.*) What?

BRIDIE: That's what someone told me. If you had a crack in your skull your brain could leak out and you'd gradually get more and more stupid.

MORAG: (*Laughing.*) Oh, Mum.

BRIDIE: That's the kind of things people said to children in those days. I believed all sorts of things for years that were pure fairy tales.

MORAG: Like what else?

BRIDIE: Oh, like if you bit your nails and swallowed them a hand would grow in your tummy. (*MORAG laughs.*) And if you kissed a boy…

MORAG: Go on.

BRIDIE: No.

MORAG: Go on, Mum.

BRIDIE: Well… If you kissed a boy and your tongue touched his, you would have a baby. (*MORAG starts to laugh.*) Yes, alright.

MORAG: Mum! (*MORAG starts to get hysterical and rolls on the ground.*)

BRIDIE: Yes, alright, clever clogs. Come on, let's get that fire built and dry your hair.

MORAG: Are they all gone?

BRIDIE: Yep.

MORAG: Are you sure?

BRIDIE: We'll do it again tomorrow just in case. Shall we put the potatoes in the fire? For a treat.

MORAG: Yeah!

MORAG goes and gets some small sticks and BRIDIE screws up pieces of paper.

BRIDIE: I bet none of your friends have real fires in the open air.

MORAG: No. Do you remember when we used to go camping to Avignon with Daddy? We had a fire every night.

BRIDIE: What did the French call potatoes in their jackets?

MORAG: Potatoes "en robe de champs".

BRIDIE: That's it. Potatoes in their dress of the fields.

While making the fire BRIDIE sings:

Sur le pont, d'Avignon, on y dans-e, on y dans-e,
Sur le pont, d'Avignon, on y dans-e, touts en ronde.

MORAG: Do you need more sticks?

BRIDIE: Yes. Lets build it high. (*BRIDIE jazzes up her singing.*)

Sur le pont, d'Avignon, on y dans-e, on y dans-e.

MORAG joins in.

Sur le pont, d'Avignon, on y dans-e, touts en ronde.

MORAG dances like Indians in a Wild West movie.

Sur le pont d'Avignon, on y dans-e, on y dans-e,
Sur le pont d'Avignon, on y dans-e touts en ronde.

MARK enters but they don't see him. They're laughing and dancing.

Sur le pont d'Avignon, on y dans-e, on y dans-e,
Sur le pont d'Avignon…

MARK: It's not *sur* le pont, it's *sous* le pont. Sous – under, under the bridge, not sur – on. (*Pause.*) So, there we are.

MORAG: (*Pause.*) We're having a camp fire, like you used to make on holiday.

MARK: So I can see. (*Pause.*) Hello, Bridie.

BRIDIE: Hello.

MORAG: We're going to put the potatoes in the fire. You can have one if you like, can't he, Mum?

BRIDIE: If he wants to.

MARK: You two could never build a proper fire. You have to put the sticks in a wigwam shape in the middle, so that the air can circulate. (*He does so.*) There.

MORAG: I knew you'd come. I knew it.

MARK: So, here you are.

MARK goes to the car. MORAG follows him.

MORAG: The car doesn't work, I'm afraid. (*MARK looks around the car.*) I don't think it would work even with petrol in it.

MARK: Ah, there's my torch. (*He takes it and pockets it.*)

MORAG: Have you got another car?

MARK: Yep.

MORAG: What?

MARK: Guess.

MORAG: A Ford Granada.

MARK: Nope.

MORAG: A Volkswagen?

MARK: Nope.

MORAG: I'll never guess.

MARK: Go on.

MORG: A Mini.

MARK: Morag!

MORAG: I don't know, tell me, please…

MARK: A Mercedes.

MORAG: Wow! What colour is it?

MARK: Red. We could go for a drive in it later…

MORAG: Can we? Mum, can we?

MARK: Maybe your mother would like to come too?

MORAG: Where is it? Can I see it?

MARK: It's down at the junction.

MORAG: I must see it. (*MORAG makes to go.*)

BRIDIE: Morag!

MORAG: Just quickly. I'll be straight back. (*MORAG exits.*)

Pause.

MARK: Well, well, well, quite a little homestead.

BRIDIE: You we're lucky to find us, actually. We're thinking of moving. But you see… Well, you know, summer's coming and… (*MARK looks about distainfully.*) Morag likes it here. She's doing very well at school. She's very good at science. Very good…

MARK: That's good.

BRIDIE: How are things with you?

MARK: Fine, fine.

BRIDIE: Still at the lab?

MARK: Oh, yes. I'm head of immunology now. I've quite a team working on my research.

BRIDIE: Good… That's good.

MARK: (*He laughs.*) I should have known you'd be here. Where I left you. (*Laughs again.*) I should have known!

BRIDIE: Don't laugh at me! Don't you bloody laugh at me! (*Pause.*)

MARK: Why did you stay here? I was waiting for you.

BRIDIE: We were waiting for you.

MARK: Yes, well here I am now. Come on, pack your things. It shouldn't take very long. I'll bring the car up. Maybe we'll just tow this lot to the scrap heap!

BRIDIE: No!

MARK: You can't live like this.

BRIDIE: Mark, I have been living...

MARK: It's time to go back, Bridie.

BRIDIE: This is our home.

MARK: Oh, don't be bloody ridiculous!

BRIDIE: You can't walk in here and...

MARK: I'm not having my wife and daughter living like... Gypsies. I never thought...

BRIDIE: No, you never did, did you?

MARK: (*Pause.*) I thought you'd be pleased to see me.

BRIDIE: Look, Mark...

MARK: Morag is.

Enter MORAG.

MORAG: It's wonderful! It must have cost a bomb!

MARK: Yes, well...

MORAG: Are we going for a drive?

BRIDIE: Um... It's a bit late now, Morag.

MORAG: Dad?

MARK: I just wanted to find out if you were okay and you're fine, so that's all right. I'll be off then.

MARK starts to exit. MORAG runs after him and clutches on to him. He extricates himself from MORAG and exits.

MORAG: What did you say to him?

BRIDIE: What?

MORAG: Don't just let him go, Mum! Let's go with him.

BRIDIE: We can't.

MORAG: Why not?

BRIDIE: Well, there's school and… What about your friends? Jenny will want to…

MORAG: I don't care. I want to go home. I want to go home! (*MORAG exits.*)

BRIDIE: Morag!

Pause. MORAG returns.

MORAG: He's gone.

Lights down.

Interval.

ACT 3

Same set. Some months later, spring. There are vegetables and daffodils growing out of old tyres and washing hanging on lines. BRIDIE is pouring beer into orange peel halves.

BRIDIE: This'll wipe the smile off their smug little faces. (*She takes the orange halves to the tyres.*) Come on my little beauties, come to Mummy.

MORAG enters playing a transistor radio with "American Pie" blaring out. She's dancing.

You're back.

MORAG: Look at what Dad bought me. Isn't it brill?

BRIDIE: (*Glancing up.*) Lovely. (*Returning to her veg.*) Come along, my darlings, have a little drinky-winky. (*To MORAG.*) Could you turn that down to deafening?

MORAG: Ah, better still! Look! (*She rummages in her pocket and takes out an ear-piece which she plugs in and the music stops.*) I can still hear the music but you can't.

BRIDIE: Good.

MORAG: You're missing out, Mum.

BRIDIE: So where have you been? (*MORAG can't hear her. BRIDIE shouts.*) Where have you been?

MORAG: Alright, Mum, keep your hair on. We went to the seaside, you'd have loved it. We went on all the rides. Dad loved it! It was magic, there were… What are you doing?

BRIDIE: Murder, Morag, murder and it feels wonderful.

MORAG: Why didn't you come with us, Mum?

BRIDIE: These lettuces are not only full of holes, they're filthy!

MORAG: We never go out, the three of us, like we used to.

BRIDIE: (*She picks some lettuces.*) What good is a slug, Morag? Horrible slimy things. (*In cowboy voice.*) There's going to be a show-down, oh, yes. It's them or us. And I knows who's a-gonna win! (*Pause.*) Who was it who died drowning in a big barrel of booze?

MORAG: What?

BRIDIE: You know, some historical chap, Dad used to go on about him. Well that's how this lot are going to meet their maker. You can come creeping out at night thinking you're going to do your evil deed and then you'll smell the booze and think: Hmm, smells good…tastes good and before you know it – plop…dead slug!

MORAG: Eugh!

BRIDIE: I might even fry them up with a bit of garlic butter and eat them for dinner. They could be nice, just like the escargots we ate in Avignon.

MORAG: You're bonkers.

BRIDIE: Might be! (*BRIDIE goes to the car. From behind it she waves a shammy leather skirt.*) Morag!

MORAG: Brill!

MORAG rushes to get the skirt and goes behind the car to try it on.

BRIDIE: (*Preparing a salad.*) You can have all sorts of things in a salad. It doesn't have to be just lettuce and tomatoes. You can have dandelion leaves, they're a bit bitter, and you can have nettles as well, you know.

MORAG: (*From behind the car.*) Get off!

BRIDIE: Why not? They're edible.

MORAG: You'd sting your mouth!

BRIDIE: Maybe you have to boil them or something.

MORAG: Can I wear it out tonight?

BRIDIE: Where are you off to now?

MORAG: I'm going to the pictures with Jenny, I told you.

BRIDIE: Oh. I thought Dad was coming back with you for dinner.

MORAG: Was he?

BRIDIE: Yes, that was the arrangement. I'm doing this salad specially.

MORAG: (*MORAG emerges.*) It's too long! I wanted it really short.

BRIDIE: Come here. (*BRIDIE takes the knife she was preparing the salad with and cuts the skirt.*) The great thing about shammy leather is that you don't have to hem it.

MORAG: What I need with this is… What's a shammy?

BRIDIE: It's some sort of a goat, I think. How's the waist?

MORAG: Fine. I wish we had a mirror.

BRIDIE: Maybe it's an antelope. Dad told me once, but I forget.

MORAG: I need some boots with this? Cowboy boots with stitching in a squiggly pattern up the side. Maybe Dad'll buy me a pair.

BRIDIE: I'm sure he will. (*Pause.*) Did he say why he wasn't coming?

MORAG: No!

BRIDIE: Typical!

MORAG: Anyway, I don't know why you want him here, you're horrible to him when he does come.

BRIDIE: No I'm not.

MORAG: Yes you are. You sit there like a moody old lump.

BRIDIE: It took him four years! And he thinks he can pick up…

MORAG: He tried to find us!

BRIDIE: You might be able to behave as if nothing's happened, but I can't.

MORAG: He looked everywhere!

BRIDIE: Oh, don't give me that!

MORAG: He did!

BRIDIE: He probably got tired of being on his own. Or nobody else would have him.

MORAG: You hate him!

BRIDIE: And you like him?

MORAG: Of course I fucking like him.

BRIDIE: Morag!

MORAG: Sorry. But you're driving me…

BRIDIE: Don't you ever use language like that!

MORAG: Sorry.

BRIDIE: Do you hear me?

MORAG: Yes. But he's my Dad, and you keep going on about him! He's still funny, he's still…he's still Dad.

BRIDIE: I know. There! (*BRIDIE's cut a bit off the length.*) That looks good, if I say so myself.

MORAG: It's still too long!

BRIDIE: You're not having it any shorter.

MORAG: That's alright, I'll fold it over at the waist.

MORAG goes to the car and gets ready.

BRIDIE: (*To herself.*) Thanks for the lovely skirt, Mum. It's great. That's alright, darling, it's a pleasure! (*Out loud.*) Do you want some salad?

MORAG: I'm going straight out. I'm not hungry. Dad bought me fish and chips and fresh doughnuts.

BRIDIE: (*Tightly.*) That was nice of him. (*She washes the lettuce in a bucket, scrutinising every leaf.*) Everything's getting dirtier. It doesn't matter how much you wash it, this stuff is deep down inside. (*She looks at some daffodils near her.*) It's on the flowers as well. It's coming off the traffic. They say that cars spew out stuff and the plants near the road get dirty. It could be poisonous.

MORAG: Get off!

BRIDIE: Honestly. They've been doing some research and there's lead or something in the plants that grow near the road and it can make you mad.

MORAG: Maybe there's some truth in it, then. (*MORAG emerges ready to go out. She's holding her stomach.*) I don't feel so good.

BRIDIE: It's all that greasy food.

MORAG: I've got a headache as well.

BRIDIE: Well don't go then.

MORAG: No, I want to.

BRIDIE: Make up your mind.

MORAG: You can listen to my transistor when I'm out, if you want to.

BRIDIE: I've plenty to do. Look at the dirt on this daffodil!

MORAG: Oh, Mum, have a break! It's the weekend. That's what weekends are for, the week ends. Your week never ends, it just rolls into the next one.

BRIDIE: That's right. (*Looking at the dirt.*) Maybe we should move.

MORAG: We could if we could get that old banger working! Maybe Dad could fix it.

BRIDIE: Dad! He has to get the AA out to change a tyre. Anyway, where would we go?

MORAG: Anywhere we wanted!

BRIDIE: Up sticks and go! I suppose we could move a little further from the road.

MORAG: We could move anywhere. Another country even.

BRIDIE: Or we could have two homes, like the swallows. This for the summer and go south for the winter.

MORAG: Yeah, go south to the sun.

BRIDIE: And be lovely and warm.

MORAG: Why not, Mum?

BRIDIE: We'll see. They haven't arrived yet, the swallows.

MORAG: They'll be here, they always are.

BRIDIE: I look for them every day.

MORAG: I'm off, Mum.

BRIDIE: Walk with Jenny to the farm gate on the way home.

MORAG: Yeah, yeah…

BRIDIE: And don't go near that main road. (*Pointing towards the audience.*) It's dangerous!

MORAG: Okay.

BRIDIE: I mean it, Morag. Take the little path and be careful and don't talk to strangers.

MORAG: God! (*MORAG exits.*)

BRIDIE: And Morag! Be careful! (*She gets a cloth and starts to wash the flowers.*) Here, let me wash your faces, your happy little faces turned up to the sun. And your hands, give me your hands. (*She washes their leaves.*) You poor little things. You sit there silently, being covered in their dirt, their smuts and you never complain. I'll wash it away, wash it all away. (*She goes towards the audience.*) Keep your muck to yourself! Look at you all speeding off to where ever you choose, happy-go-lucky, with us in your wake! (*She walks back to the car.*) Up sticks and go! (*She kicks the poles away from the awning.*) Why not!

She picks up the beer bottle for the slugs and drinks from it. She looks at the salad and flings it on the floor. She kicks over the bucket and then the flowers. She starts to cry. She collects herself and starts to put the soil back in the pots. Enter MARK.

MARK: Hello, Bridie, I…what's happened here?

BRIDIE: (*Tidying.*) Oh, it's nothing, nothing, it's just…

MARK: Who did this?

BRIDIE: Look it doesn't matter, I'll have it back to normal in no time.

MARK: Did Morag do this?

BRIDIE: No… Well… It doesn't matter…she doesn't mean anything by it.

MARK: (*Sternly.*) Where is she?

BRIDIE: It's alright. She's gone out

MARK: Wait till I see her!

BRIDIE: Leave it, Mark.

MARK: Where's she gone?

BRIDIE: I don't know!

MARK: She just wanders off, does she?

BRIDIE: That's right.

MARK: How do you put up with it?

BRIDIE: I'm used to it! (*Pause.*) Look leave it, I think it's best we don't say anything to her.

MARK: I'll decide if I say something or not. I had no idea she was behaving like a…like a drop out. But of course, that's how you live.

BRIDIE: It's funny, I used to dream of you coming back and me having all the things I've missed. But do you know what? I don't miss your restaurants or your cars, or your money.

MARK: Fine!

BRIDIE: Yes, fine. We were doing fine.

MARK: (*Looks about.*) Oh, yes!

BRIDIE: Yes. I found other things here, Mark. Things you wouldn't know anything about. Things you can't buy.

MARK: Good. I'm pleased for you! And I'm happy to leave you to it. But I don't want my daughter living like a tinker. Do you hear?

BRIDIE: You turn up here in your fat Mercedes and whisk her…

MARK: And you can't stand it, can you?

BRIDIE: If you love her so much, why did you walk out on her?

MARK: Oh, don't start that again! Look at this place! Look at this! (*He kicks the tyres.*) Weeds growing in tyres!

Enter MORAG unseen by MARK and BRIDIE. He pulls the washing off the line.

Rags hanging everywhere! I can give her things! Proper things!

BRIDIE: When it suits you!

MARK: A proper home! This is a dump!

MORAG: It's not a dump! It's not! It's not! (*Seeing the mess.*) What have you done to it? (*MORAG tries to put the awning back.*)

MARK: I haven't done…

BRIDIE: Why aren't you at the pictures?

MORAG: My tummy ache's got worse.

BRIDIE: Here, sit down, darling,

MORAG: You're rowing again, aren't you?

MARK: Your mother and I are trying to sort things out.

MORAG: No you're not. You're screaming at each other.

MARK: Adults talk to each other like that, sometimes. You'll understand when you're a bit older. It's not as bad as it looks.

MORAG: I can't stand it!

BRIDIE: Alright, Darling.

BRIDIE comforts MORAG. MARK and BRIDIE exchange incriminating looks.

MORAG: Why can't you two… Oww… (*She holds her tummy.*)

BRIDIE: What is it, darling?

MARK: Does it hurt a lot?

MORAG: Bit.

BRIDIE: Why don't you lie down, sweetheart and see how you are?

MORAG nods. MARK helps her to the car with BRIDIE.

MORAG: Okay, I'm okay. Where's my radio?

MARK: It's here, look. (*He gives it to her.*) And your ear-piece.

BRIDIE: I'm just outside if you want me.

MORAG: Okay. (*She settles down.*)

MARK: I'm here too, Monkey.

MORAG: Okay.

MARK and BRIDIE sit together in silence.

BRIDIE: Are you alright, pet?

No answer. BRIDIE goes and looks in the car and then returns to MARK.

She's curled up with her transistor.

MARK raises his eyebrows. Pause.

MARK: (*Indicating to the mess.*) Who did this? (*BRIDIE doesn't answer.*) Did you do it, Bridie?

BRIDIE nods. Pause.

BRIDIE: What did you do?

MARK: What?

BRIDIE: When we weren't there. I mean…what do you do with your time?

MARK: I go to work.

BRIDIE: And?

MARK: I go to work. I'm free to do whatever I like.

BRIDIE: And that's what you wanted, isn't it? (*MARK goes and looks in the car.*) Is she alright?

MARK: I think she's asleep.

BRIDIE: Is she breathing?

MARK: Yes!

BRIDIE: (*Dramatically.*) Are you sure? How can you tell?

MARK is about to speak and then realises BRIDIE's joking, they laugh with the shared memory. It's getting dark.

MARK: She looks so little curled up there. You know, Bridie, when I was her age I was wandering around Europe.

BRIDIE: I know.

MARK: "A displaced person". No Mama. Papa in a prison camp.

BRIDIE: I know, Mark.

MARK: Ah, but I never told you this. I had walked all the way through Austria, almost to freedom, when I missed my father so much, do you know what I did? I walked back to find him.

BRIDIE: Back where?

MARK: He was in a prison camp in the Ukraine. I had been walking for weeks, months. Go west, Papa had said, follow the sun. Sun rises in the east and sets in the west, but the further I walked from home, the emptier I felt. I came to the top of a hill and ahead of me was freedom. I looked at it, turned round and headed back. But there was no home left, of course. I met a priest, he gave me some soup, thin soup, with lumps of fat floating on the top, it would turn my stomach now. It was the best meal I'd ever eaten.

BRIDIE: Did you find him?

MARK: Huh?

BRIDIE: Your Papa?

MARK: Oh, yes, I found him. I'll never forget his face when he saw me through the wire. Can you imagine? "What are you doing here?" he said. "You can't come in here."

BRIDIE: So what did you do?

MARK: I turned round and set off again, walking in a daze, to nowhere. Alone, except for… (*He takes out his mouth organ.*) of course.

BRIDIE: It must have been hard on your Papa, seeing you like that.

MARK: Do you know, Bridie. I've never thought about it.

BRIDIE: Did he ever speak about it, after the war?

MARK: Nope. I think we were all just grateful to have survived.

He starts to play "What a friend I have in Jesus" and then breaks off.

I always think of Papa as a hero, on his white horse. He was always so brave, strong, silent. I never think of him frightened or sad or lonely.

BRIDIE: He must have been.

MARK: I always feel that I ran away and he stayed and fought.

BRIDIE: You were a child.

MARK: I know. But I didn't know that at the time.

BRIDIE: You were brave too.

MARK: It didn't feel like it. Running, hiding, stealing…

BRIDIE: Do you want something to eat?

MARK: Huh?

BRIDIE: I was going to do a salad or something.

MARK: Go on then.

BRIDIE goes to the car and looks at MORAG.

BRIDIE: I know I had a life before I had her, but I think of that woman as a different person, do you know what I mean? (*MARK starts to play and breaks off.*) Go on. I was enjoying it. Do you remember when I lived in Earls Court and you used to serenade me under my window? (*BRIDIE starts to laugh.*) And my landlady threw a bucket of water over you. (*BRIDIE picks up the bucket.*) "Stop that caterwauling or I'll…" (*She looks at the bucket.*) Oh, no! There's a hole in this. All the water's run out!

MARK: (*Singing.*) There's a hole in my bucket, dear Liza, dear Liza,
There's a hole in my bucket, dear Liza, a hole.

BRIDIE: Then fix it, dear Henry, dear Henry, dear Henry,
Then fix it, dear Henry, dear Henry, fix it.

MARK: With what shall I fix it, dear Liza, dear Liza?
With what shall I fix it, dear Liza, with what?

BRIDIE: With straw, dear Henry, dear Henry… Is that the song? With straw?

MARK: I think so.

BRIDIE: Isn't that strange? How can you mend a bucket with straw?

MORAG: (*From the car.*) Mum! Mum! Come here a minute will you.

BRIDIE: What is it dear? (*She goes to the car.*)

MORAG: (*From the car.*) Look! What is it? Am I dying? What is it?

MARK: What's the matter?

BRIDIE: It's alright, Mark. You're not dying, darling. It's normal. It's part of being a woman.

MARK: Oh, God!

BRIDIE gets into the car and looks after MORAG. MARK plays the mouth organ. BRIDIE emerges from the car with MORAG wrapped in a blanket.

MORAG: That's awful!

MARK: Thanks a lot!

BRIDIE: It's not awful… It's…it's special. (*MORAG pulls a face. All three sit down together.*) It means you can have children.

MORAG: I don't want to have children!

MARK: Well not quite yet, maybe, but…

MORAG: I feel sick.

BRIDIE: It's alright, it's everything churning up inside you. (*Pause.*) Look at that lovely full moon.

MARK: Did you watch the moon landing?

BRIDIE: No.

MARK: It was fantastic.

BRIDIE: It's funny to think that a man has walked on the moon.

MARK: I might be able to get you a bit of moon dust, Morag.

MORAG: Honest?

MARK: That would be something to take into school, wouldn't it?

MORAG: Yeah!

BRIDIE: Is it safe?

MARK: Of course it's safe!

BRIDIE: I read something about viruses or something.

MARK: Don't be ridiculous.

BRIDIE: People don't know. It's another world up there.

MORAG: Will you stay tonight? (*MARK and BRIDIE exchange looks.*)

MARK: I'd love to, but there isn't any room.

BRIDIE: (*To MORAG.*) Come on you, bed.

MARK: Yes. I'll see you soon.

BRIDIE helps MORAG to the car.

MORAG: Night, Daddy.

MARK: Night, poppet. See you, Bridie.

BRIDIE: Night, Mark. Drive safely.

Exit MARK.

Now, darling, how are you feeling?

MORAG: A bit better.

BRIDIE: You snuggle down there.

MORAG snuggles down in the car. BRIDIE sits down near by. Pause. BRIDIE looks up at the moon and sings:

I see the moon and the moon sees me…

MORAG: (*From the car.*) Mum! Do you think Daddy can really get me a bit of the moon?

BRIDIE: Oh, yes, darling, oh yes.

Lights down.

ACT 4

1976. Summer. Same set. Bright sunlight. BRIDIE, wearing an old summer smock, is under the awning putting tomato chutney into jars. A cassette player plays Frank Sinatra singing "Three Coins in a Fountain". It is drowned out by the roar of a motorbike. BRIDIE runs towards the sound. We hear the sound of breaks. Enter MORAG. She is wearing ski pants, stilettoes and red lipstick, carrying a duffel bag. The motor bike roars off.

BRIDIE: You're going to kill yourself!

MORAG: Might! (*She kicks off her stilettoes.*) Dad not here yet?

BRIDIE: No.

MORAG: God! I really rushed!

BRIDIE: Your Dad hates that boy.

MORAG: It's stock taking at the shop. We had to count every record, every LP. They're still all over the floor (*Hearing the music.*) What that? It's awful! (*She turns it off.*)

BRIDIE: I was enjoying that.

MORAG: (*Picking at the chutney.*) Is this for tea?

BRIDIE: Don't do that!

MORAG: I'm starving!

BRIDIE: This is for the roadside table.

MORAG: Eurgh!

BRIDIE: It's doing rather well, actually.

MORAG: We nearly knocked it over with the bike. (*MORAG tries to get her chair under the awning.*) I can't believe Dad's not here yet. They let me and the other

70

Saturday girls go early but I think the rest of them will be there all night.

BRIDIE: Sit over there!

MORAG: I've got to sit in the shade, I'm boiled!

BRIDIE: There's cold lemonade in the bucket.

MORAG gets some lemonade from the bucket and puts on some flip flops.

MORAG: Look, the grass is going all brown and dusty. I've never seen it like this. They're putting up stand pipes for water in the streets.

BRIDIE: Really?

MORAG: They're talking about rationing it. They're saying 76 is going to be the hottest summer on record. Do you fancy a bit of T Rex?

BRIDIE: No, thanks.

MORAG takes Cosmo *out of her bag.*

MORAG: Is there any bread?

BRIDIE: We'll eat when Dad gets here.

MORAG: Ohh! (*Browsing through her mag.*) Is he having his food and then pissing off?

BRIDIE: Morag!

MORAG: That's what he usually does. I wanna go to the drive-in movie place. They've set one up, on the football pitch. Open air, like the ones in America. I thought I might go there tonight.

BRIDIE: Oh, Morag!

MORAG: I can go later on when Dad goes.

BRIDIE: And who are you thinking of going with?

MORAG: (*Reading.*) Who do you think?

BRIDIE: (*Tuts.*) Tearing around the countryside with that biker!

MORAG: He's not a biker! He just happens to own a motorbike. Have you ever been on a motorbike, Mum?

BRIDIE: No.

MORAG: No. Well, you should try it. It's fantastic! It's better than being in a car, there's no glass between you and the world.

BRIDIE: It's dangerous.

MORAG: Danny's bought me my own motorcycle helmet.

BRIDIE: Good.

MORAG: Well, it's not completely mine, it's for his passengers. But I'm his main passenger so I'll be the one wearing it. It's beautiful! It's black and shiny and looks like a bowling ball with a window in it.

BRIDIE: Are you and Danny going out?

MORAG: (*She laughs.*) No!

BRIDIE: Tell me the truth.

MORAG: No! Anyway, what if we were? Most of the girls in my class have got boyfriends.

BRIDIE: Jenny hasn't.

MORAG: Hmm, not through lack of trying. (*Pause.*)

BRIDIE: It's illegal.

MORAG: (*Laughs.*) What?

BRIDIE: It's illegal in this country until you're sixteen.

MORAG: What are you talking about?

BRIDIE: You know what I'm talking about.

MORAG: Oh! Sex! Sexy sex, sex! I wasn't talking about sex. (*She reads.*) So, in five weeks' time I can have sex can I?

BRIDIE: In five weeks' time you get your O-level results and then…

MORAG: And then?

BRIDIE: Next year is an important year for you at school. You should be thinking about that, not…Danny!

MORAG: Danny says there's a road in Italy that's right on the edge of the cliffs and it goes on for miles with the sea crashing below. He went biking there. He says it's the most beautiful road in Europe and there are little cafés clinging to the cliffs and you can sit there eating your pizza, watching the sun go down. He's going to go back there this summer.

BRIDIE: No.

MORAG: What?

BRIDIE: No, you're not going to Italy with Danny.

MORAG: I didn't say I was, did I?

BRIDIE: No, but you're not anyway. (*Pause.*) I'm serious, Morag. Dad says you've got to decide what you want to do at university.

MORAG: What's it got to do with him?

BRIDIE: He's your father.

MORAG: Hello? Dad? I can't see him.

BRIDIE: It's the sort of decision a family makes together.

MORAG: (*She laughs.*) I agree.

BRIDIE: Good.

MORAG: If we had that sort of a family. (*BRIDIE starts to put up a folding table.*) Why don't we ask Dad to take us out for dinner?

BRIDIE: Oh, I don't think I want to…

MORAG: We could go to the Little Chef.

BRIDIE: I don't want to get dressed up.

MORAG: Mum, it's the Little Chef, not the Savoy.

BRIDIE: No. You know what I mean. Anyway, I've made a lovely salad.

MORAG: (*Pulls a face.*) Come on, Mum, let's go out! You need to. You've been wearing that horrid old smock for weeks.

BRIDIE: So?

MORAG: So!

BRIDIE: What's wrong with it?

MORAG: Just saying. (*She reads.*) Here you are, Mum, do the *Cosmo* quiz with me. It's a good one for you: Are You a Secret Screen Goddess? (*BRIDIE is staring at MORAG's ear.*) Mum! Are you a Monroe, or a Bette Davis?

BRIDIE: Neither. I'm a mother. It's septic!

MORAG: What?

BRIDIE: Your ear.

BRIDIE goes to touch MORAG's ear stud.

MORAG: Get off!

BRIDIE: It's all red around the stud.

MORAG: It's meant to be like that. Listen. (*She reads.*) You know a guy fancies you but he hasn't asked you out. Do you…

BRIDIE: It can't be meant to be like that! There must be dirt in there.

MORAG: Mum!

BRIDIE: It could be dangerous.

MORAG: Do you: A.) Wait for him to ask you out, however long it takes?
B.) Pretend you've won two tickets for the cinema and…

BRIDIE: I don't know why you want to mutilate yourself.

MORAG: I think it's beautiful and I'm going to get some pearl studs.

BRIDIE: Why not diamond ones?

MORAG: Why not?

BRIDIE: I hope this Danny's rich.

MORAG: Listen: Do you: A.) Wait for him to ask you?
B.) Pretend you've won two tickets for the cinema? OR
C.) Jump into bed with him at the first opportunity?

BRIDIE: What!

MORAG: A, B or C? (*BRIDIE takes the magazine.*)

BRIDIE: This stuff's filth!

MORAG: Oh, Mum, it's…

BRIDIE: "Jump into bed with…"!

MORAG: It's just a quiz. Give it back!

BRIDIE: No!

MORAG: Give it back, it's Jenny's! (*MORAG grabs the magazine.*)

BRIDIE: Putting ideas into your head! If your father sees it he'll go mad.

MORAG: It's just a magazine! Come on, next question…

BRIDIE: No! It's not what you should be thinking about.

MORAG: Right, what do you think I should be thinking about?

BRIDIE: Your A-levels! Your future!

MORAG: What do you want me to do? Sit here on a chair thinking about my future? Right! (*MORAG sits bolt upright on a chair with her eyes closed.*)

BRIDIE: It's not a joke, Morag. I want you to have the opportunities I didn't have.

MORAG: I don't want your opportunities, Mum. (*Pause.*) Alright then, what about you, what about your future? When I go, the world's your oyster!

BRIDIE: Horrible slimy things.

MORAG: No! Think about it, Mum. Are you going to stay here? What about you going to college?

BRIDIE: Don't be ridiculous!

MORAG: Why not?

BRIDIE: I'm too old.

MORAG: There's lots of old people studying nowadays.

BRIDIE: What for?

MORAG: Because they want to, I suppose, I don't know. What are you going to do? Make chutney? You could live for fifty years! That's a hell of a lot of chutney. In fifty years' time, Mum, you're going to be creeping around here in your smock, with your spuds and your tyres and you'll be all on…

We hear a motorbike arriving. MORAG runs towards the sound.

BRIDIE: It's him again, isn't it?

MORAG: Yeah! (*MORAG waves.*)

BRIDIE: What's he want?

MORAG: I don't know.

Exit MORAG.

BRIDIE: (*Shouting.*) Your Dad's coming!

BRIDIE takes out a table cloth and puts it on the table. She looks in the car window at her smock and her reflection.

Cheeky cow! (*Imitating MORAG.*) Creeping around in your smock, with your spuds...

We hear the sound of the bike going. BRIDIE sits down disconsolately. She puts the Sinatra back on. "Witchcraft" starts to play. She starts to hum along and act out the lyrics: "Those fingers in my hair, that sly come-hither stare ..." She goes to the car and fixes her hair in the car wing mirror. The music gets into her. She brings some cutlery to the table. She picks up the table cloth and wraps it around her shoulders 50's film star-style. She takes off her smock.

She's wearing solid foundation garments. She wraps the cloth around her and moves to the music shimmying and dancing. She sees MORAG's stilettoes, takes off her trousers and puts on the stilettoes.

She goes back to the car and rummages about in the back seat. She takes out her dress from Act One. Puts it on. Gets MORAG's red lipstick from her hand bag. Puts it on in the car mirror and continues to dance.

When the music ends she turns it off and sits where she was at the beginning. Pause. She puts three plates of salad on the table.

MARK enters carrying a take away.

MARK: You're never going to... (*He stares at BRIDIE.*)

BRIDIE: What?

MARK: You're all dolled up!

BRIDIE: Oh, this, oh, yeah. I was tidying up and I er… found it. What have you got there?

MARK: It's a Tandoori. (*He puts the foil containers on the table and opens them up.*)

BRIDIE: A what?

MARK: It's all the rage in London. I didn't think I'd get it up here. It's chicken cooked in a special oven called a tandoor.

BRIDIE: It's bright red!

MARK: It'll go well with the salad. I think you might like it.

BRIDIE: Go on then. (*They serve it up.*)

MARK: Shall we wait for Morag?

BRIDIE: She's been and gone.

MARK: Where's she gone?

BRIDIE: I don't know. Right. (*She eats.*)

MARK: She knew I was coming!

BRIDIE: Oh, Mark. (*Pause.*) Hmmmm, this is delicious!

MARK: Great, isn't it?

BRIDIE: I didn't think I'd like it.

MARK: I knew you would.

> *Pause. BRIDIE looks at MARK; they become aware that it's the two of them at dinner.*

BRIDIE: I've made some new tomato chutney.

MARK: Oh, yes.

BRIDIE: The tomatoes are very tasty, like the ones we used to get. I've added a bit of green pepper.

MARK: Really.

BRIDIE: Yes. I've made twenty jars.

MARK: How many?!

BRIDIE: For my table. (*Pause.*) This is really very good. It's doing rather well. There was £2.56 in the jar this morning. (*Pause.*) How's work?

MARK: Oh, fine, fine. We're still on the Variola Major vaccine.

BRIDIE: That's nice.

MARK: It's very exciting. I think the W.H.O. is going to irradicate small pox. It's taken two hundred years since Jenner created the first vaccine in 1796, but we're getting there.

BRIDIE: Lovely.

MARK: What do you think of that, Bridie? A world without small pox.

BRIDIE: Amazing!

MARK: If it is eradicated, we're going to store some of the virus.

BRIDIE: Whatever for?

MARK: Well we don't want to wipe it out!

BRIDIE: I suppose not.

Pause.

MARK: Morag out with gypsy-boy, is she?

BRIDIE: He's not a gypsy.

MARK: I've seen him. He's got a ring in his ear.

BRIDIE: He's not a gypsy.

MARK: Oh, you like him do you?

BRIDIE: I don't… I don't know him. More salad? (*She takes it off MORAG's plate.*)

MARK: Thanks. I suppose they're on the bike. When I think of my daughter speeding up and down the motorway on a kitchen chair… Doesn't it worry you, her out on that thing?

BRIDIE: Yes, Mark, it terrifies me! What do expect me to do, lie down in front it when they're driving off! (*Pause.*) It's funny, I never pictured Morag as a grown up.

MARK: She isn't one.

BRIDIE: No, I mean… When I looked at her as a baby, I could imagine her becoming a little girl, and what she'd look like, but I never imagined her as an adult. I look at her sometimes now and think, "who are you?".

MARK: Do you remember when she was a baby we used to stare at her? I loved her so much I wanted to eat her up.

BRIDIE: She hardly remembers a thing about being little. I've asked her. She remembers coming here, but even that's a bit hazy. It's as if that was our time not hers. She'll be gone soon.

MARK: Not for a while.

Pause.

BRIDIE: When I was young, I never thought about getting old.

MARK: That's because you were young.

BRIDIE: I think about it all the time now.

MARK: That's when you know you're old. And it's too late then.

BRIDIE: Sorry?

MARK: You can't go back.

BRIDIE: They say that it's never too late, don't they?

MARK: (*Pause.*) It is for some things.

BRIDIE: I better get those jars out. That really was delicious. I've got some bags somewhere. (*She loads the jars into carrier bags.*)

MARK: I've been thinking, maybe Morag would like a holiday. What do you say?

BRIDIE: Well, she wants to go to Italy.

MARK: Then I'll take her.

BRIDIE: Hmm. I think she wants to go with Danny.

MARK: What!!

BRIDIE: No, no, she hasn't said anything definite, but I think she'd like to.

MARK: Out of the question!

BRIDIE: She's nearly sixteen.

MARK: She's not going anywhere with that yobbo!

BRIDIE: She's got to go out.

MARK: What, to Italy?

BRIDIE: (*We hear the motorbike.*) Well, you have a talk to her then. (*Exit BRIDIE with the bags. MARK goes and hides behind the car. MORAG enters smoking.*)

MARK: (*Emerging.*) Take that disgusting thing out of your mouth.

MORAG continues smoking.

Did you hear me, Morag?

MORAG: I hear you.

MARK: Nicotine, in its pure form, is one of the most powerful poisons known to man.

MORAG: Good.

MARK carefully takes the cigarette from her and slowly stubs it out.

MARK: It's also used as an insecticide. That's nice, isn't it? If you want to kill yourself why take so long about it? There are plenty of faster acting poisons.

MORAG: Where's Mum?

MARK: Doing something with her chutney. (*Pause.*) Morag, you are fifteen…

MORAG: Nearly sixteen.

MARK: Nearly sixteen. Society has deemed that at fifteen, nearly sixteen, years of age you are not experienced enough to make considered choices. Like this boy you've been going around with…

MORAG: Oh, here we go.

MARK: We don't know anything about him.

MORAG: For God's sake, Dad…

MARK: What does he do for a living?

MORAG: He's a brain surgeon, alright?

MARK: Good. That's the sort of man you deserve. That's the sort of boyfriend that your mother and I…

MORAG: He's not my boyfriend.

MARK: I know all about you and him.

MORAG: (*Shouting.*) He's not my boyfriend!! He thinks I'm funny and sweet and a good mate, but doesn't want to be my boyfriend! (*She bursts into tears.*)

MARK: Oh. Look…

MORAG: It's because I'm too boring!

MARK: Don't be ridiculous!

MORAG: I am. The other girls are wilder and more…wild, and I'm…nothing.

MARK: That's not true.

MORAG: It is, Dad. It is! I'm frightened of everything. Mum and I, we're so frightened. Things that go bump in the night, strangers, men. And now I'm going to be stuck here for ever in this place. (*MORAG sobs.*)

MARK: Come here. (*MARK gingerly puts his arm around her.*) I know you've got a funny little home, Monkey. It's a higgledy-piggledy sort of ramshackle place…

MORAG: I thought he really liked me.

MARK: He's young. He doesn't know what he likes. You're a very special girl and anyone who can't see that is blind, do you hear me? And if this fellow can't see that, well it's his problem. Any more trouble from him and he'll have to answer to me. (*MARK jumps up in a boxer pose. Fists raised.*) You haven't seen your Daddy in action, have you? Oh yes, Queensbury rules and all that! Take that, you cad! You bounder! (*He boxes.*) Upsetting my little girl. Come on! Put up your paws! Hah! He'd run away, Morag!

MORAG: (*Laughs a little.*) He sure would, Dad.

MARK: Oh, yes! (*He gives her a hanky.*) That's more like it. Come on, dry your eyes.

MORAG: I loved riding on the bike.

MARK: A bike, what's a bike? I'll get you a bike. I'll buy you the biggest bike that has ever been seen. And you'll ride it like a chariot and people will think you're Boadicea and they'll gasp and they'll point and say: "Look! There goes Morag the Great, daughter of Mark the Great, grand daughter of Papa the Great!" (*MORAG laughs.*) People will come and go in your life, Morag, but nobody will love you like your parents.

MORAG: You're never here, Dad.

MARK: I'm here now. And listen. I'm not Mark the Great, I know that, but your Grandpapa really was Papa the Great. When the tanks rolled into Warsaw all they had was horses, beautiful white horses, but what good are they against the might of the tanks? But did that stop Grandpapa? Everyone was panicking, everyone was screaming. Warsaw is fallen, the eagle has lost its crown. Do you know what Papa did? He put on his colonel's uniform, his long black boots, his shining silver spurs, and his sword and he strode down the street. People were so frightened, they shouted from windows, they told him to hide, run and hide. He walked on down the street, into the stables. Some other members of the cavalry were there. He asked for his horse, that's all he said and he mounted it. And the strangest thing happened, other men called for their horses. Nothing was said. No plans made. They rode out of the stable, a small group of them. They rode through the streets, hooves on cobbles, bridles jangling, metal sparkling and as they drew near the tanks they broke into a trot. Soon they were only yards away from them and Papa drew his sword and shouted: "Charge!". They rode hell for leather at the tanks! Right into them. People will do anything, smash through anything for freedom. Never forget that.

MORAG: Did he die?

MARK: What do you mean? You met him, don't you remember?

MORAG: Oh, sort of…

MARK: You must remember and you must never forget because that's who you are, Morag, deep down, that's who you are. He wasn't frightened, he wasn't hiding under a stone. And he helped other people to have courage and to believe in themselves. So, Morag the Great, don't ever tell me you're nothing, do you hear? (*MORAG nods.*) Your life's ahead of you, live it!

Enter BRIDIE. She sees MARK and MORAG.

BRIDIE: Everything alright?

MARK: Oh, yes. Morag was a bit upset, but we had a little chat and she's alright now, aren't you, Monkey?

MORAG: I'm fine. (*She goes to the car.*)

BRIDIE: Did you have a word with her?

MARK: What? Yes, yes, she's fine.

BRIDIE: There was another three pound twenty in the chutney jar.

MARK: Great! Look, I better be off.

BRIDIE: Oh, okay. See you soon then.

MARK: Oh, I didn't mention the holiday to her. Will you suggest it?

BRIDIE: I will, I will.

MARK: It might be good for us all. We could drive. How about it? Through France, Germany and Austria, over the mountains to Italy. All of us together, in the car, like the old days.

BRIDIE: Yes, maybe.

MARK: Right.. I'm off. (*He kisses BRIDIE on the cheek. She's shocked.*) See you, Morag!

MORAG: (*From the car.*) See you, Dad.

Exit MARK.

BRIDIE: Did Dad go on at you a bit?

MORAG emerges out of the car with her duffel bag.

MORAG: It was fine.

BRIDIE: He cares about you, that's all.

MORAG: You've got my shoes on.

BRIDIE: Oh, yes. Here.

MORAG: No, it's alright, I'll wear these. (*She puts on some sensible shoes.*)

BRIDIE: Are you going to the drive-in? Oh, look the swallows, they're back! How do they do that, how do they find their way?

MORAG: Nobody knows.

BRIDIE: It must be built-in.

MORAG starts to leave the stage, walking into the audience/ traffic.

Don't go that way!

MORAG charges through the audience into the darkness. We hear a loud screech of breaks.

Morag!!!

Pause.

MORAG: I'm alright, I'm alright, I'm alright!

BRIDIE: What are you doing?

MORAG: I've got to go, Mama, I've got to go! I love you, I love you very much but I've got to do something, I've got to…

BRIDIE: Wait!

MORAG: I can't…

BRIDIE: It's dangerous, Morag, it's dangerous. You don't understand…

MORAG: Love you, Mama. (*Exiting.*)

BRIDIE: Come back!

MORAG exits from the auditorium.

My baby.

The lights fade on BRIDIE.

The End.

THEATRE 503 AT THE LATCHMERE

Opened as part of the Gate Theatre in 1982 and re-launched in 2002 as a theatre dedicated to new writing and the new generation of emerging playwrights, Theatre 503 at the Latchmere has quickly established itself as one of the most dynamic and exciting new writing venues in London.

'The tiny Latchmere Theatre…is carrying the torch for new writing and developing an enviable reputation for spotting the potential of playwrights at the start of their careers.'
The Guardian, *November 2003*

Since 2002 Theatre 503 at the Latchmere has staged over twenty new plays by important new writers including Phil Porter, Ursula Rani Sarma, Jennifer Farmer, Ronan O'Donnell, Samantha Ellis, Glyn Cannon, Peter Morris, Trevor Williams, Said Sayrafiezadeh, Falk Richter, Anna Marie Murphy as well as new plays by more established playwrights such as Ron Hutchinson, Naomi Wallace and Fraser Grace.

'Consistently unearthing some of London theatre's most exciting new voices.' Time Out, *April 2003*

Artistic Director	Paul Higgins
Associate Directors	Johnnie Lyne-Pirkis
	Phil Hewitt
Literary Associate	Matthew Morrison
Artistic Associate	Jessica Beck
Theatre Administrator	Anna Bewick

Winner of The Empty Space Peter Brook Theatre Award 2004

Plays premiered at Theatre 503 at the Latchmere and published by Oberon Books include *Touched… / Blue* by Ursula Rani Sarma, *Stealing Sweets and Punching People* by Phil Porter, *Debris* by Dennis Kelly and *Ministry of Pleasure* by Craig Baxter. All Oberon titles are available from **www.oberonbooks.com**.

www.ingramcontent.com/pod-product-compliance
Ingram Content Group UK Ltd.
Pitfield, Milton Keynes, MK11 3LW, UK
UKHW031252020325
455690UK00007B/80

9 781840 025262